THE GLENCOE LITERATURE LIBRARY

Study Guide

for

Walk Two Moons

by Sharon Creech

New York, New York   Columbus, Ohio   Woodland Hills, California   Peoria, Illinois

To the Teacher

The *Glencoe Literature Library* presents full-length novels, nonfiction, and plays bound together with shorter selections of various genres that relate by theme or topic to the main reading. Each work in the *Library* has a two-part Study Guide that contains a variety of resources for both you and your students. Use the Guide to plan your instruction of the work and enrich your classroom presentations.

In **For the Teacher** you will find these timesaving instruction aids:
- *About the Work*: pertinent background information on the work, including a character list, a plot synopsis, key themes, and an annotated bibliography
- *Media Links*: annotated listings of audio, visual, electronic, and print resources related to the work
- *Teaching Options*: high-interest activities for introducing the work and individualizing instructions
- *Assessment Options*: alternative assessment activities for greater flexibility in evaluating students' understanding of the work
- *Options for Using Related Readings*: suggested approaches to the Related Readings included with the work
- *Answer Key* and *Assessment Rubrics*: detailed answers to all questions and reading activities and evaluation for alternative assessment activities

For the Student consists of these reproducible blackline masters:
- *Meet the Author*: a lively overview of the author's life
- *Introducing the Work*: background information that provides a meaningful context in which to read the work
- *Before You Read* and *Responding pages*: pre- and post-reading questions and activities
- *Active Reading*: graphic organizers for students to complete as they read
- *Test*: a comprehensive two-part test of the work

NOTE: This novel focuses on the concerns of many contemporary readers. Certain words, references, or situations may offend some readers.

Photo Credit
Page 13: Courtesy HarperCollins

Glencoe/McGraw-Hill
A Division of The McGraw·Hill Companies

Copyright © The McGraw-Hill Companies. All rights reserved. Permission is granted to reproduce material contained herein on the condition that such material be reproduced only for classroom use; and be provided to students, teachers, and families without charge; and be used solely in conjunction with *Glencoe Literature*. Any other reproduction, for use or sale, is prohibited without written permission of the publisher.

Send all inquiries to:
Glencoe/McGraw-Hill
8787 Orion Place
Columbus, OH 43240

ISBN 0-07-825321-7
Printed in the United States of America
1 2 3 4 5 6 7 8 9   045   05 04 03 02 01

Contents

For the Teacher

- **About the Work** — 2
  - Character List — 2
  - Synopsis — 2
  - Major Themes in the Novel — 3
  - Approaches to Teaching the Novel — 3
  - Further Reading for the Teacher — 3
- **Media Links** — 4
- **Teaching Options** — 5
  - Options for Motivating Students — 5
  - Meeting Individual Needs — 6
- **Assessment Options** — 7
- **Options for Using Related Readings** — 8
- **Answer Key** — 10
- **Assessment Rubrics** — 12

For the Student

- **Meet Sharon Creech** — 13
- **Introducing the Novel** — 14
- **Chapters 1–11**
  - Before You Read — 16
  - Active Reading — 17
  - Responding — 18
- **Chapters 12–22**
  - Before You Read — 20
  - Active Reading — 21
  - Responding — 22
- **Chapters 23–33**
  - Before You Read — 24
  - Active Reading — 25
  - Responding — 26
- **Chapters 34–44**
  - Before You Read — 28
  - Active Reading — 29
  - Responding — 30
- **Related Reading Blackline Masters** — 32
  - All My Relations by Linda Hogan — 32
  - from Pa-ha-sa-pah or The Black Hills of South Dakota by Rev. Peter Rosen — 33
  - the little horse is newlY by E. E. Cummings — 34
  - The Tide Rises, the Tide Falls by Henry Wadsworth Longfellow — 34
  - Five Rounds by Lorenzo Baca — 35
  - Celebration by Alonzo Lopez — 35
  - Moon by Chaim Potok — 36
- **Test** — 37

About the Work

WALK TWO MOONS BY SHARON CREECH

Sudden death and the grieving process are not subjects that lend themselves to humor. In *Walk Two Moons*, however, Sharon Creech addresses a child's profound sense of loss in a novel that is often richly funny. In a voice that is homespun and true, Salamanca ("Sal") Hiddle, Creech's thirteen-year-old narrator, captures the peculiar behavior of family and friends as she travels west, following the journey her mother took before losing her life in a bus accident. Only at the journey's end is Sal fully able to accept the finality of her mother's death. And only at the novel's end does the reader grasp the significance of the relationships between the characters and the incidents that occur along the way. Published in 1994, this poignant, comic novel—the author's second book for young adults—won the 1995 Newbery Medal.

Students will immediately respond to Sal's quirky observations and colorful speech. Note, however, that the novel is rich with idioms and regional colloquialisms that may prove especially challenging for less-proficient students and English-language learners. Note also that the story's numerous flashbacks and use of the frame technique may challenge this population as well.

CHARACTER LIST

Salamanca Tree Hiddle, the thirteen-year-old narrator who cannot accept her mother's death until she retraces her steps on a journey to Idaho
Mr. Hiddle, Sal's grief-stricken father
Gram Hiddle, Sal's exuberant, eccentric grandmother who dies on the trip to Idaho
Gramps Hiddle, Sal's colorful grandfather and Gram's devoted husband who drives his wife and Sal on the journey west
Margaret Cadaver, Mr. Hiddle's friend and confidante who was Sal's mother's seatmate during the bus accident that claimed her life
Phoebe Winterbottom, Sal's imaginative friend whose mother, under strange circumstances, leaves her family
Mr. Birkway, Margaret Cadaver's brother who is Sal's and Phoebe's English teacher
Mrs. Winterbottom, Phoebe's respectable mother who keeps a secret about her past from her family

SYNOPSIS

For reasons that are unclear to Sal Hiddle, her mother left the family farm in Kentucky for Lewiston, Idaho, and did not return. Sal's grief-stricken father rents out the farm that Sal loves and uproots her to Euclid, Ohio, a suburb of Cleveland. Sal hates her new home and cannot accept her father's disturbing relationship with red-haired Margaret Cadaver, a nurse who has persuaded Mr. Hiddle to move to Ohio for work. Sal refuses to believe that her mother will never return.

That summer, Gram and Gramps Hiddle, Sal's paternal grandparents, take her on a six-day car trip from Euclid to Lewiston, Idaho. Sal's goal is to reach their destination on Sal's mother's birthday. The trio travels westward, retracing the route taken by Sal's mother.

To pass the time, Sal recalls the events that preceded her mother's departure and at Gram's insistence, narrates a tale of her experiences in Euclid that past year. At the heart of the story is Sal's friend Phoebe Winterbottom's grief over her mother's sudden disappearance. The imaginative Phoebe insists that her mother has been kidnapped by a lunatic.

Phoebe's loss parallels Sal's loss, and Phoebe's story brings Sal's into sharper focus. The mystery is solved when Phoebe's mother returns home with the "lunatic"—a son whom she gave up for adoption years before and whom her family has not been told about.

Sal's story does not have a similar happy ending. Gram is dying of a stroke, and Sal has driven herself to Lewiston to visit the scene of her mother's death.

The reader finally understands that Sal's mother, who had suffered from an identity crisis, had set out for Idaho to find herself. When the bus in which she was riding careened off the road in Lewiston, all of the passengers died except for Margaret Cadaver, the last person to have seen Sal's mother alive.

The journey ends, Gram's body is sent back to Kentucky for burial, and Gramps, Sal, and her father return to their beloved farm in Kentucky.

MAJOR THEMES IN THE NOVEL

Several themes run through *Walk Two Moons*. Three prominent ones are the error of prejudging, the maturation process as a journey, and the interconnectedness of life.

The error of prejudging. The novel's title is derived from the adage, "Don't judge a man until you've walked two moons in his moccasins." The error of prejudging is conveyed by Sal's determination to dislike Margaret Cadaver without really knowing the truth about her. In chapter 4, Sal says, "Somehow it was easier to deal with Margaret if there were reasons not to like her, and I definitely did not want to like her."

The maturation process as a journey. At the beginning of the novel, Sal describes her dislike of her new environment and cannot understand why her father uprooted her from her beloved Kentucky. By the end of the novel, Sal appreciates what she has learned from Phoebe and her family. In chapter 44, she says, "Phoebe and her family helped me, I think. They helped me to think about and understand my own mother."

The interconnectedness of life. For Sal the natural world possesses a spirit that can heal her wounds. On her way west, she prays to the trees for her mother's return. Sal treasures the idea that her mother's spirit has returned to nature. In chapter 42, she tells the sheriff, "She isn't actually gone at all. She's singing in the trees."

APPROACHES TO TEACHING THE NOVEL

- Teach *Walk Two Moons* with a focus on the **frame**, or story-within-a-story, technique. Explain that the main plot concerns Sal's journey west and her ultimate acceptance of her mother's death. This plot is the frame for the parallel story that Sal tells her grandparents about her friend Phoebe's mother's disappearance. Invite students to identify parallel situations in each story, and ask them to consider why these similarities are important.
- Teach the novel with a focus on the coming-of-age genre. Explain that coming-of-age novels are those in which characters experience conflicts that force them to make decisions that lead to their maturity. Ask students to recall and describe coming-of-age stories that they have read or seen on TV or in the movies.
- Teach the novel with a focus on the **first-person point of view**. Point out that in a story narrated from the first-person point of view, the narrator is one of the characters, referred to as "I." The reader experiences events through that character's eyes. Students should consider the narrator's relationship to the other characters and whether the narrator's interpretation of events and of other characters' motivations is reliable.

FURTHER READING FOR THE TEACHER

- "Newbery Medal Acceptance" by Sharon Creech and "Sharon Creech" by Lyle D. Rigg, *Horn Book*, July/August 1995. In her acceptance speech Creech discusses the origins of *Walk Two Moons*. An affectionate profile of the author by her husband, Lyle D. Rigg, follows.

Media Links

 Videos

- The following videos may help students better understand the characters, cultural context, theme, and setting of the novel.
- *The Education of Little Tree* (1997, 112 minutes), rated PG; a coming-of age story about an orphaned Cherokee who is raised and tutored by his grandparents in the Smoky Mountains of the 1930s and meets difficulties after he is forced to attend the Notched Gap Indian School.
- *Homecoming* (1996), with Anne Bancroft; rated PG; a drama about a family of four children who are deserted by their mother and who are reluctantly taken in by their stern grandmother.
- *Mt. Rushmore and the Black Hills of South Dakota* (30 minutes), explores sites visited by Sal on her journey, including the Badlands.

 Art

The following paintings can be used to engage students in a discussion about the status of the Native American people in U.S. society, past and present.
- *American Progress* by John Gast, 1872, shows an idealized "Spirit of Progress" floating over a plain filled with advancing wagons, trains, and parties on foot, while Indians and buffalo flee before them.
- *Buffalo Road III – Choices* by contemporary Native American artist G. Peter Jemison, illustrates, in the style of a collage, the choices that today's Native Americans must make between the traditional and modern ways of life.

 Audiocassettes

- *Walk Two Moons*, read by Kate Harper, presents the complete novel on four cassettes. An abridged version, read by Mary Stuart Masterson, is also available on audiocassette.

Internet Connections

Students interested in learning about Yellowstone National Park can visit *The Total Yellowstone Page* at **http://www.yellowstone-natl-park.com/index.html**
This site provides a wide variety of information—from geysers and service stations to the latest wolf sightings.
- A comprehensive index to Native American Internet resources—including history, culture, language, and art—can be found at **http://www.hanksville.org/NAresources/**.

At the time this Study Guide went to press, the Web sites were in operation. Before assigning students to visit the sites, check to ensure that the sites still exist.

 Further Reading for the Student

- *American Indian Myths and Legends*, selected and edited by Richard Erdoes and Alfonso Ortiz, Pantheon Books, 1984. The stories in this collection are arranged by themes—including creation myths, trickster tales, monsters, animals, ghosts, and heroes.
- *How It Feels When a Parent Dies* by Jill Krementz, Alfred A. Knopf, 1988. Eighteen young people, each of whom have lost a parent, tell of their sorrow and healing.
- *Absolutely Normal Chaos* by Sharon Creech, 1995, Creech's first novel for young readers that concerns adolescent themes.

Be sure to preview all media links to determine whether the material is appropriate for your class.

Teaching Options

Options for Motivating Students

The Color of Words

Acquaint students with the colorful language of the novel.
- Explain that *Walk Two Moons* includes a number of colorful words and expressions that reflect the cultural background of the characters. List a few on the board and ask students what they think they mean: "whangdoodle," "Trying to catch a fish in the air," and "a hog's belly full of things."
- Invite students to share colorful words or expressions that their parents or grandparents use in everyday speech. Make a list of these on the board. Have students explain to the class what these words and expressions mean and why they enliven the language.
- Explain that an expression whose meaning cannot be translated from the meanings of the words that compose the expression is an idiom. For example, "spin a yarn" is an idiom. Encourage students to keep a list of idioms and colorful expressions as they come across them while reading.

Tree of Life

Prepare students for the significance that trees play in the novel's setting.
- Write the word *tree* on the board. Invite students to make a word web naming the kinds of trees that grow where they live and the ways in which they enhance the quality of life.
- Explain to students that the setting in which a story takes place contributes to the tone of the story. Point out that trees are such an important part of the novel's setting that the narrator's name includes the word *tree* and her mother's name means sugar maple.
- Encourage students to look for references to trees throughout the novel. Have them jot down these references as they read. Then have them explain the significance of the tree as a symbol in the novel.

Judge Not...

Help students relate their own experiences to the experiences of the characters in the novel.
- Have students record in their journals an instance in which they prejudged a person and the judgment proved to be wrong. On what was the prejudgment based? How did they find out that they had misjudged the person? What lesson did they learn from the experience?
- Encourage students to look for instances in *Walk Two Moons* in which one character prejudges another and is proven to be wrong.

Sacred Places, Sacred Spaces

Introduce students to the importance of sacred places for communities or individuals.
- Point out that some cultures have places that are sacred to them. These may be buildings, such as the Kaaba in Mecca—sacred to Muslims—or large territories, such as the Black Hills of South Dakota—sacred to the Sioux nation.
- Suggest that there are also places that are sacred to us as individuals—places where we retreat for inner peace or spiritual refreshment. Have students think of their own sacred places and invite them to share with the class why that place is important to them.
- Explain that sacred places exist in *Walk Two Moons*. Encourage them to look for these places as they read and to note why they are significant.

Meeting Individual Needs

The suspenseful plot and informal tone of Walk Two Moons *make it appropriate for average readers. The following activities are designed to help you present the novel in ways that meet the needs of all students.*

Less-Proficient Readers

Help students understand the structure of the novel's plot.

- Explain to students that two story lines run through the novel. The first concerns what happens to Sal on her trip west to Idaho. The second is the story of Phoebe Winterbottom that Sal tells her grandparents to pass the time on the journey.
- Point out that when Sal is not describing the unusual antics of Gram and Gramps or recalling the mysterious goings on in Ohio, her mind drifts back to the time her mother left the farm in Kentucky, never to return. This unfolds in a series of flashbacks that are not told in chronological order.
- Pair gifted students and less-proficient students to work in small groups. After students have read a chapter, have groups discuss the events that occurred and their significance to the story.

English-Language Learners

Encourage students to use contextual clues and to read for overall meaning.

- Explain that the narrator does not always tell her story in conventional English and that a few of her friends and relatives express themselves in original ways—even to the extent of making up words. Explain further that the meanings of some of the expressions are not clear even to native English speakers.
- Remind students that they need not understand every word or expression to understand the story. Encourage students to read for overall meaning and not word-for-word meaning. Suggest that they listen to the audiotape (see Media Links, page 4) as they read along in their books. Tell students to bookmark pages on which they encounter unfamiliar words and expressions. They can return to those pages to use contextual clues to determine the meaning.
- Explain to students that idioms are exceptions to this rule and cannot always be understood by using contextual clues.
- Pair students who have difficulty reading English with students who are more fluent with the language. Encourage the partners to discuss each chapter after they read it.

Gifted and Talented

Challenge students to respond to literary criticism.

- Inform students that *Walk Two Moons* won the prestigious Newbery Medal in 1995, and that the Newbery Medal is awarded annually by the American Library Association for "the most distinguished contribution to American literature for children." Point out that the novel was considered to be a controversial choice. The author, who lives in England, was virtually unknown in the United States, and her book was criticized both for its subject matter and its technique.
- Distribute to students copies of the following excerpt, taken from a rather negative review in the *New York Times*, May 21, 1995:

  All the women characters turn out sweet and good and a bit peculiar. All the men too—the fathers, the teacher, the boyfriend, the police, even the thief. By the end of the novel this noble 13-year-old decides that maybe her mother left to set her daughter free. Everything is pat; hope is shining. We have what John Leonard calls the formula of "goodwill, coincidence and pluck."

- Have students discuss in groups the criticisms raised in this review. Then ask them to write a response, focusing on the question of the author's characters and overall theme.

Assessment Options

Writing

On the Road to Discovery
- Have students write an essay in which they compare and contrast the process of discovery that Sal experiences in *Walk Two Moons* and that Moon experiences in *Moon* by Chaim Potok. Point out that discovery is an important part of the maturational process and can be about oneself, others, or the meaning of life.

Parallel Worlds
- Have students write an essay analyzing the parallel stories that characterize the plot of *Walk Two Moons*. Suggest that they review the Venn diagram they completed as part of the **Active Reading** section on page 29. Ask students to explain in their essays the relationship of Phoebe's world to Sal's and its importance in the development of Sal's self-knowledge.

A Tragicomedy?
- In a critical essay, ask students to discuss the tone of *Walk Two Moons*. Would they define this as a comic novel, a sad novel, or a little of both? In their essays, have students include examples illustrating how the author achieves the effect that she does. Finally have students give their opinions on whether the author succeeds in establishing a singular tone.

Listening and Speaking

Underage Driver
- Pair students to role-play the scene in which Sal is stopped by the sheriff after taking Gramps' car to visit the scene of the accident where her mother was killed. One student should assume Sal's role, and the other that of the sheriff. Students should work together to develop a script for each role.

Viewing and Representing

Westward Ho!
- Point out that by referring to a map of the United States that shows interstate highways, students can follow the route from Euclid to Lewiston. Encourage students to use clues provided in the narrative that identify specific locations in states along the route. Then have pairs of students create a map that shows the route that the Hiddles take to Idaho. They should use enlarged photocopies, or create a map of their own, indicating important stops along the way and locating approximately where the travelers spent each night. Students should illustrate their maps with pictures or appropriate quotations from the novel.

Home Sweet Home
- Have students create a scene that features key elements of the landscape of Bybanks, Kentucky, as it is described by Sal. Students should look throughout the novel for vivid descriptions of the place and try to capture the scene artistically, using whatever media they deem suitable. Students can display their artwork if they wish.

Interdisciplinary Connection

Geography/Math: Map It!
- Have students use a map of the United States that shows interstate highways that lead from Euclid, Ohio, to Lewiston, Idaho. Using the scale of miles on the map, they should estimate the distance in miles between the two points and then convert the figure to kilometers.
- Students may wish to evaluate whether Internet directions represent an efficient route and whether it follows the same route taken by Sal.

Social Studies: Head for the Black Hills
- The history of the Black Hills of South Dakota is a fascinating study. Have students research this tragic era and report what they learn to the class.

 Save your work for your portfolio.

Options for Using Related Readings

Related Readings	Making Connections to *Walk Two Moons*
All My Relations by **Linda Hogan** (BLM page 32)	**Sal's mother is proud of her Native American heritage. Her feelings of kinship with nature is central to the sweat lodge ceremony described in this essay.** • You may wish to use this essay as a prereading activity for the novel. • Pre-teach the following difficult vocabulary: *foci, permeate, purveyors, crux, skeletal,* and *lithe.* • Before they read this selection, ask students what they know about Native American spirituality. Afterward, invite them to share what they have learned. Encourage them to look for themes of healing and nature as they read the novel. • Point out that tobacco was believed to have both medicinal and spiritual attributes in traditional Native American society and that smoking was an important part of religious ceremonies. • After reading, ask students to suggest reasons a person might want to participate in a sweat lodge ceremony. What personal event may have impelled the author to become "part of something larger"?
from ***Pa-ha-sa-pah*** or ***The Black Hills of South Dakota*** by **Rev. Peter Rosen** (BLM page 33)	**Sal realizes what it must have been like for the Native Americans to lose their land. This description, written in the nineteenth-century, offers a sympathetic account of such a loss.** • You may wish to use this selection as a prereading activity for chapter 28 of the novel, when Sal and her grandparents arrive in the Black Hills. • Pre-teach the following difficult vocabulary: *aught, kindle, profusely, vernal, incarceration, fabulous, repugnance, encroachment, strata,* and *edifices.* • Explain to students that in 1868, the second Treaty of Fort Laramie guaranteed the Sioux nation sixty million acres of land known as the Great Sioux Reservation, including the Black Hills. Yet the discovery of gold and the white settlers' appetite for land soon overturned the agreement. The Indians' destruction of General George Custer's army in 1876 led to their own swift defeat. By 1881, when Sitting Bull surrendered to the authorities, South Dakota belonged to the white man. • Ask students to infer the attitude of Rev. Peter Rosen to events that took place in the twenty years before his account (1875–1895). Encourage them to identify passages and phrases that convey his sympathy with the Native American people. Ask students to compare Rosen's attitude to that of Sal's.

Related Readings	Making Connections to *Walk Two Moons*
the little horse is newlY by E. E. Cummings **The Tide Rises, the Tide Falls** by Henry Wadsworth Longfellow	These contrasting poems are both introduced in the novel. Sal's response to them suggests that they each reflect a side of her personality. • You may wish to use these selections as a postreading activity for chapter 29 of the novel, when Phoebe reports her mother's disappearance to the police. • Invite volunteers to read the Cummings poem aloud in a way that conveys the most meaning. Remind students that Sal liked the sound of the phrase "smoothbeautifully folded," although she was not sure what it meant. Suggest that the sound of a poem often contributes to its sense. • Point out that the reader is in the same position as the little horse: Just as the horse must make sense of his new environment, so the reader must try to make sense of the poem. • Help students understand that sound is an important element of the Longfellow poem as well. Invite a volunteer to read it as it is read in the novel. Ask students if they agree with Megan or Sal. Is the poem gentle or terrifying? Why?
Five Rounds by Lorenzo Baca **Celebration** by Alonzo Lopez (BLM page 34)	These Native American poems have as their themes the all-embracing cycle of life. Sal comes to find solace in this view of the world. • You may wish to use these selections as a postreading activity to formulate the theme of the novel. • Help students to understand how the circle, a universally accepted symbol of continuity, is used to describe many natural processes. Have them define phrases such as *life cycle*, *water cycle*, and *cycle of the seasons*. Point out that Sal returns to the farm in Kentucky, where her life began. • Suggest that the circle is a symbol that represents wholeness. Remind students that the novel's most joyful character is Gram, who shouts "Huzza, huzza" from the center of a Native American circle dance. • Have students experiment with concrete poems of their own. Suggest that they begin with a visual concept and then create the words to fit the idea.
Moon by Chaim Potok	Moon, a middle-class American boy, finds his values challenged by a young anti-child labor activist from Pakistan. The empathy that springs from knowledge is also a theme of *Walk Two Moons*. • This selection could be used as a prereading or postreading activity for the novel. • Ask students what they know about the source of the things they take for granted: jeans, soccer balls, shoes, and produce from the supermarket. Discuss with them how knowledge about the origin of such items might influence their habits. Read to them the following quote from Iqbal Masih (the model for Ashraf in this story): "the world's two hundred million enslaved children are your responsibility." • Encourage students to compare and contrast Moon and Ashraf. • Have students consider how Moon changes over the course of the story. Invite them to predict what he will do in the years after the events described in this story take place.

Answer Key

ACTIVE READING
Chapters 1–11
A: Gramps pulls off the Ohio Turnpike and botches an attempt to fix a woman's car. B: Sal has dinner with Phoebe's family. A: Gramps, Gram, and Sal stop to wade in Lake Michigan; they spend a night near Chicago. B: A stranger comes looking for Mrs. Winterbottom; a mysterious message arrives at Phoebe's door. A: Sal visits Madison, Wisconsin, and the Wisconsin Dells. Gram dances with the Indians. B: The Winterbottoms receive another strange message, and the girls see the lunatic again.

Chapters 12–22
Sample answers: *Angry:* draws doodle of Mrs. Cadaver hanging; *Observant:* notices how Phoebe takes her mother for granted; *Sad:* remembers her mother's last day on the farm; *Loyal:* supports Phoebe when her mother leaves; *Loving:* understands her father's misery; *Imaginative:* believes that a tree can sing; *Unreasonable:* doesn't want to hear the truth about Mrs. Cadaver

Chapters 23–33
Mystery: Why is the sky so high? *Myth That Explains It:* People made long poles and pushed the sky as high as they could. *Mystery:* Where did fire come from? *Myth That Explains It:* Prometheus stole fire from the Sun and gave it to humanity. *Mystery:* Why is there evil in the world? *Myth That Explains It:* Pandora, out of curiosity, opened a beautiful box that Zeus had sent to man, and evil was released into the world.

Chapters 34–44
Sal's story: mother loses baby; mother tells family that she's leaving; Sal goes on long journey; has loving grandparents; had to move home; has no siblings; *Phoebe's story:* mother leaves a note that she is leaving; mother brings back a son; family knows mother is alive; Phoebe informs police of the disappearance; Phoebe tracks down her mother; receives mysterious messages; *Sal's and Phoebe's story:* girls very miserable; girls have unrealistic ideas about mothers; girls learn about mothers

RESPONDING CHAPTERS 1–11
Recall and Interpret
1. Stated reasons: They are going to see the country. Sal is good at reading maps. Real reasons: Gram, Gramps, and Sal all want to see Sal's mother. Dad wants to be alone with Margaret Cadaver. The real reasons are probably too painful to talk about.
2. Sal is angry and resentful toward Mrs. Cadaver. Students may say that it is because she does not want her mother to be replaced.
3. Both the Winterbottoms and the Pickfords are polite and respectable. Sal does not seem to find them likeable. The Pickfords mouths turn down at the corners. The Winterbottoms are picky about their food.
4. Phoebe does not follow the advice. She assumes that the young stranger is a lunatic, and she believes that Mrs. Cadaver has done something "diabolic" to her husband.
5. The author has created suspense by shrouding Mrs. Cadaver, the lunatic, and the origin of the messages in mystery. Readers also are in suspense as to what Sal will find in Idaho.

Evaluate and Connect
6. She tells the story to keep her mind off of her mother's leaving. Students' comparisons to their own experiences will vary.
7. Students may say that Sal's flinching when she is touched suggests that, as a result of her mother's absence, she withdraws from close human contact.

RESPONDING CHAPTERS 12–22
Recall and Interpret
1. Gram and Gramps' bed is the object that they value most. It suggests that their relationship is loving and stable.
2. Sal understands that Mrs. Winterbottom is miserable. She might be conscious of it because she remembers her own mother's unhappiness.
3. When she hears the bird, Sal remembers the singing tree in Kentucky. Gram may think that Sal's spirits are lifted.
4. Sal's mother wishes people would call her Chanhassen, her real name. She leaves home to learn about who she is. She may think that using her real name would be a first step.
5. The note says that Mrs. Winterbottom is going away for a while. It reminds Sal of her own mother's departure.

Evaluate and Connect
6. Ratings will vary. Students may say that the relationship was loving but that Mrs. Hiddle needed time to herself.
7. Responses will vary, based on students' webs. Some may say that Sal's mother did not have a clear idea of who she was.

RESPONDING CHAPTERS 23–33
Recall and Interpret
1. Sal broke her leg, and her mother carried her to the house. Sal feels that she may have been responsible for her mother's losing the baby.
2. Sal sees Mary Lou's parents kissing. She is reminded of her own parents.
3. Pandora's box explains how evil came into the world. The story affects Sal because she can't understand why she has suffered such pain.
4. The poem tells about a man who drowns in the rising tide. Sal understands the poem's theme of sudden loss.
5. Sal learns that Mr. Cadaver died suddenly in a car accident. She begins to sympathize with Mrs. Cadaver.

Evaluate and Connect
6. Phoebe, like Sal, is grieving over the loss of her mother. Because Sal identifies with Phoebe, she is able to overlook Phoebe's behavior and remain a loyal friend to her.
7. Some students will likely say Phoebe is a believable character because her anger is a natural reaction to her mother's sudden disappearance.

RESPONDING CHAPTERS 34–44
Recall and Interpret
1. Sal worries about driving off the road. She is thinking of her mother's fatal accident.
2. Sal learns that Ben's mother is in a psychiatric hospital. The fact that their mothers both had emotional difficulties might bring the two closer together.
3. Mr. Winterbottom realizes that the wife he had known had been concealing her real personality. This reminds Sal of her own mother's struggle to find herself.
4. Moody Blue pushed her puppies away so that they would become independent. Sal feels that her mother had wanted her to become independent too.
5. Sal finds her mother's grave. At last she is able to accept the reality of her mother's death.

Evaluate and Connect
6. Some students might say that Sal would have gotten over her grief earlier if she had gone with her father. Others may say that she was not yet ready to accept the truth.
7. Comparisons will vary. Some students may say that Sal's grief is overly drawn out; others may find it realistic.

Answer Key *(continued from previous page)*

RELATED READINGS

All My Relations
1. The author visits to make arrangements for the sweat lodge ceremony.
2. She must bring fifty tobacco ties, wood, meat, and bread.
3. "All my relations" refers to all people and to the natural world. It is an important phrase because it emphasizes the key themes of the ceremony: relating with others and the wholeness of creation.
4. The author realizes that she is not alone because she is "part of something larger."
5. In telling Phoebe's story to Gram and Gramps, Sal begins the healing of the pain she feels at her own mother's loss.

from Pa-ha-sa-pah or The Black Hills of South Dakota
1. White settlers entered the territory, building towns and villages. The train, the telegraph, and the telephone aided their advance.
2. The effect of the list is to show the abundance of animal life in the earlier days and to stress how things have changed.
3. They felt resentful. They told a story about a white giant who was imprisoned in a mountain for invading their land.
4. Rocks are shaped like tall buildings, and, from a distance, mountain sheep resemble people.
5. Sal sympathizes with the Native Americans. If they had asked her for their land back, she says she would have given it to them.

the little horse is newlY; The Tide Rises, the Tide Falls
1. The horse's world is beautiful, fresh, amazing, fragrant, bright, and welcoming.
2. Students may suggest that the joyful innocence of the little horse is a quality possessed by young children.
3. The traveler drowns in the rising tide. The sea "calls" the traveler, and the waves erase his footprints. He never returns to shore; this suggests that he has drowned.
4. "The Tide Rises, the Tide Falls" implies a world full of unexpected danger. No hint of such menace is found in "the little horse is newlY."
5. Sal has a joyous personality as depicted in the Cummings poem. She loves nature, stories, people, and words. Her mother's death was sudden and unexpected, as was the traveler's in Longfellow's poem.

Five Rounds; Celebration
1. The second and third poems can be read as complete sentences.
2. The words run together, encouraging the reader to repeat them, like a wheel turning on itself.
3. The mood is joyful. Words such as *feasting, leaps, stomps, laughter,* and *games* contribute to this feeling.
4. The speaker dances in circles, the form in which "Five Rounds" is written. Both poems suggest unity and wholeness.
5. Like the circles featured in these poems, Estsanatlehi's life never ends; it rotates like a wheel.

Moon
1. Things that make Moon angry include his parents' talking about him as if he were absent, being called Morgan, being told to keep his door open, and being interrupted by call waiting on the telephone. He controls his anger by breathing deeply and counting slowly.
2. Ashraf talks about boys in Pakistan being bought by factory owners. Moon is startled by the revelation.
3. Ashraf plays very intently. He sweats and his eyes glow like coals. Playing bongos might be Ashraf's way of releasing tension and anger.
4. Students might say that they learned that Moon is serious and compassionate. He is furious about the death of Ashraf and relieves his anger by playing the drums passionately at the memorial assembly for him.
5. When Moon learns about Ashraf's struggles and realizes that they both share a common interest, he stops being self-centered and begins to think about others.

TEST

Recall and Interpret
1. b   2. d   3. a   4. c   5. b
6. Sal's father wants to leave the farm because of its constant reminders of his wife. Sal is angry and does not want to leave.
7. Sal remembers that Phoebe is unable to see that her mother is unhappy with her life. She realizes that both she and Phoebe do not want to accept the truth.
8. Sal once saw her mother kiss a tree after eating some blackberries. Later that day, Sal kissed the same tree and tasted blackberries. After that, all trees tasted of blackberries to Sal.
9. Mr. Winterbottom shakes Mike's hand and welcomes him to the family as his son.
10. Sal does not want to see that a bird is responsible for the singing. She wants to believe that the tree itself is singing, as though it contained the spirit of her mother.

Evaluate and Connect (any 2)
1. Students should understand that Gram and Gramps are giving Sal the opportunity to come to terms with her mother's death. Along the way she learns that her mother was troubled by feelings of inferiority and failure and she needed to be alone to find out who she was. Sal realizes that her mother was an individual who was trying to find herself and was in no way rejecting Sal.
2. Students may choose from a number of characters or incidents. Among them are 1) Mrs. Cadaver, who seems to be standing between Sal and her father; 2) the lunatic, who seems to be harassing the Winterbottoms; 3) Mrs. Winterbottom, who seems very respectable; 4) the messages, which seem to be coming from the lunatic; 5) the boy at the river, who seems to be a liar; 6) Sal's mother, who seems to be a carefree farmer's wife.
3. Students should understand that in thinking about Phoebe, Sal learns that her mother was an individual in her own right, who needed an identity apart from the one given her by her family.
4. Responses may suggest that the singing tree is a symbol of the survival of the human spirit after death or the unity of humankind and nature. The marriage bed can be viewed as a symbol of a loving, enduring relationship—the kind that Gram and Gramps shared. The hidden fireplace might represent the false appearances that hide the truth in life.
5. Students' responses will vary. Some may find that the characters are fully realized and believable because many come across as being original. Others may find the characters' antics unbelievable. Students may not agree that the novel is contrived in certain instances. They may argue that the details of plotting are not as important as the self-knowledge that Sal gains at the end. Some may argue further that deception is one of the book's key themes.

Assessment Rubrics

Use the following criteria as guidelines for evaluating students' performances on Assessment Options activities presented in this Study Guide.

Writing

On the Road to Discovery
- The essay includes a thesis statement that identifies the two principal characters and summarizes points of comparison and contrast in their discovery process.
- The student clearly explains similarities and differences, using specific examples from the respective works.
- The student uses transitional words and phrases to make relationships clear.
- The essay demonstrates competency in grammar, mechanics, and usage.

Parallel Worlds
- The student's thesis statement concisely summarizes the relationship of the subplot to the plot and its importance to Sal's self-development.
- The student selects relevant details from the text to support his or her thesis.
- The details are organized effectively.
- The student observes the conventions of grammar, usage, and mechanics.

A Tragicomedy?
- The student establishes the novel's tone in a concisely worded thesis statement.
- The student supports his or her arguments with specific evidence from the book.
- The student uses logical reasoning when expressing an opinion.
- The essay ends with a statement of the student's opinion about the author's success in establishing a distinct tone.

Listening and Speaking

Underage Driver
- Students' scripts should be based on the facts presented in the novel.
- Students' dialogue should be believable and appropriate to the situation.
- Presentations should be well rehearsed and confidently performed.

Viewing and Representing

Westward Ho!
- Students effectively use the clues provided in the novel to establish the route traveled by Sal and her grandparents.
- Students' maps clearly and accurately identify important locations along the route.
- Students' quotations or illustrations are aptly chosen to correlate with the journey.

Home Sweet Home
- Students' scenes should depict a vividly described landscape.
- Students' pictures should accurately portray what is stated or implied in the description.
- Students' pictures should reflect creativity and imagination.

Interdisciplinary Connection

- Students' estimates should fall within a reasonable range of a hundred miles.
- Students should be able to cite their source verifying the estimate.
- Students should be able to defend their opinions of the accuracy and efficiency of the Internet map that they choose as a resource.

Head for the Black Hills
- The student demonstrates an understanding of western frontier life during the late nineteenth century.
- The student is able to bring his or her information to life in an oral report.
- The historical details that the student uses are relevant and interesting to the audience.
- The student's presentation is well organized and adequately rehearsed.

Meet Sharon Creech

When I was young, I loved books, although I couldn't tell you the titles of books I've read. It was more the experience of reading that was so memorable—to be able to be all those different people. I could be a boy, I could be a girl. I could be an Indian or a Greek warrior. Eventually, I thought it had to be the greatest thing in the world to be able to make up all those things.

—Sharon Creech, "An Interview with Sharon Creech, 1995 Newbery Medal Winner," *The Reading Teacher*, February 1996

Sharon Creech describes how, as a girl growing up in Cleveland, Ohio, she had to compete with "hordes of relatives telling stories around the kitchen table." If you weren't good enough, she explains, "your story was drowned out by someone else's more exciting one."

Slow to Start Despite her practice as a storyteller, Creech was slow to becoming a published writer. Born in 1945, she was educated at Hiram College and George Mason University in Washington D.C. Creech wanted to write plays but instead remained in Washington, working at a dull job that she describes as "all politics and facts."

A Break with the Past In 1979 Creech made a complete break with her past life by going to teach at a school for American students near London, England. As a single parent with two children, she had to persuade the principal that she could handle the job. It was there that her writing skills bore fruit. According to her future husband, Creech's letter of application "was a masterpiece of persuasion."

Fame as a Writer Creech loved teaching and began to write with imagination and passion. Two novels for adults were followed by a book for young readers—*Absolutely Normal Chaos*. The flow of ideas was by now unstoppable: the kitchen-table stories had found their way onto paper. "I've always thought that there were too many ideas and not enough time to sit down and develop them," she once remarked.

With *Walk Two Moons*, Creech's second novel for young people, she achieved sudden fame. It happened one day in 1995 when her writing was going particularly badly. She went out into the backyard at her home in England to scream. The telephone rang. Expecting the message to be about a typical school emergency, she was surprised by the news that she had won the Newbery Medal for the year's best novel for young readers. "Every time I think of that phone call I get the shivers," she recalls.

Laughter and Tears Critics praise Creech's clever plots and eccentric characters and admire her ability to write about the most serious subjects with wit and humor. Her first four novels for young readers include deaths that affect the central characters directly, yet each employs lighthearted language and joyous imagery that evoke smiles from readers in spite of the subject matter. It may be Creech's ability to write about serious subjects in a way that makes readers laugh that contributes to her popularity with readers of all ages.

Creech still lives in England, but in the summers she returns to the United States to join her relatives who are "all part of a big, noisy, crazy family."

Introducing the Novel

When I began to write, I was living in England and I was missing the States. I was also missing my grown children who had just gone off to college there. I wrote Walk Two Moons *from the notion of a parent/child separation, and I decided to do it from the child's point of view. These were the kinds of things rolling around in my mind.*

"An Interview with Sharon Creech, 1995 Newbery Medal Winner," *The Reading Teacher,* **February 1996**

BACKGROUND

Where does a writer get ideas for an imaginative novel like *Walk Two Moons*? Often they spring from his or her own experiences. In the quotation above, Sharon Creech tells why she wrote about separation. She hadn't actually lost her two children, but they were far away and she missed them. Like Sal, the narrator of *Walk Two Moons*, Creech was grieving. "I know that her longing is also my longing," she writes of Sal. "I was living an ocean away, longing for my children, my larger family, and for my own country."

Several of the themes and incidents in *Walk Two Moons* stem from Creech's life. In the novel, thirteen-year-old Sal takes a journey with her grandparents from a Cleveland, Ohio, suburb to Lewiston, Idaho. This is the same trip that Creech took the summer that she turned twelve. The journey remains a vivid memory for her: "What a journey! What a country!" she recalls. "What spectacular and unexpected sights reared up around each bend!" Longing for her mother, Sal is not so enthusiastic about the trip, but her grandmother echoes Creech's excitement.

During the trip west, the family stopped at an Indian reservation and bought Creech a pair of moccasins for her birthday. She was thrilled because she loved reading Native American stories. A cousin of hers had told her that one of their ancestors was an Indian. "I loved that notion," Creech explains, "and often exaggerated it by telling people that I was a full-blooded Indian." Similarly, in *Walk Two Moons*, Sal is proud of the fact that she is part Indian.

The Indian myths that Creech loved best involved reincarnation—the belief that a person returns to life after death, usually in another form. "How magnificent and mysterious to be Estsanatlehi, the 'woman who never dies'," she writes. "I wanted to live a thousand, thousand lives." Not surprisingly, the theme of reincarnation plays a major role in *Walk Two Moons*. Sal takes comfort in the belief that her mother's spirit inhabits a beautiful "singing tree."

The book's title has an unusual origin. One day the author broke open a fortune cookie in a Chinese restaurant. The message read, "Don't judge a man until you've walked two moons in his moccasins." Below it were the words "American Indian proverb."

THE TIME AND PLACE

The year in which the action of *Walk Two Moons* occurs is never disclosed. The omission may be because the author sought to give the novel a sense of timelessness.

If the time of *Walk Two Moons* is uncertain, however, the places are not. Euclid, Ohio, is a real city located northeast of Cleveland. Further, during the trip west, they stop at several well-known places of interest. Among them are

- **Pipestone National Monument, Minnesota**
- **Badlands National Park, South Dakota**
- **Black Hills, South Dakota**
- **Old Faithful, Wyoming**
- **Lewiston, Idaho**

The map on the next page shows the route that Sal and her grandparents travel, including their main stops along the way.

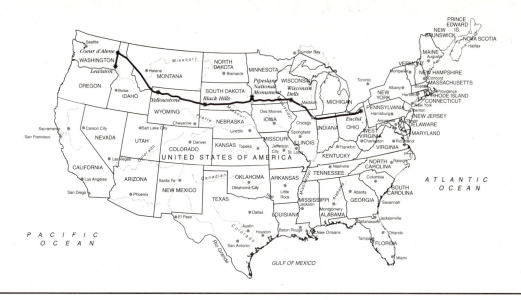

Did You Know?

The Ohio Turnpike, which Sal describes in chapter 2 as "the flattest, straightest piece of road in God's whole creation," is one of several roads that has been built in the eastern United States since the late 1700s. They were built as profit-making ventures. Turnpikes originated in England in the mid-1600s, when the Parliament permitted private companies to maintain roads and to charge tolls for their use. The term *turnpike* comes from the name of a revolving frame bearing spikes that served as a barrier to vehicles entering the road. After the driver paid the toll, the pike was turned to allow passage. In the United States, many turnpikes failed to make a profit and were turned over to the county for control by 1850. Besides the Ohio Turnpike, other major turnpikes include the Massachusetts Turnpike, the New Jersey Turnpike, the Pennsylvania Turnpike, the New York State Thruway, and the Indiana Toll Road.

CRITIC'S CORNER

The following excerpt is from a review of Walk Two Moons *that appeared in the New York Times, May 21, 1995:*

> It's great that the hero on the archetypal quest here is a young woman in search of courage and identity. . . . As Sal retraces her mother's steps through the Badlands and the Black Hills, she tells stories about her friend's mother, who also left, and we learn Sal's mother's story and her grandparents' story and her own. The storytelling is comic and affectionate, each chapter building to its own dramatic climax. Sal's voice is sometimes lost and lonely, expressing her grief and also her awe for the great country she's traveling through. We recognize that she's been stuck physically and emotionally. She learns that "a person couldn't stay all locked up in the house. . . A person had to go out and do things and see things."

Before You Read

Walk Two Moons Chapters 1–11

FOCUS ACTIVITY

Think of a time when you took a long trip by car or bus. What was the purpose of the trip? How did you pass the time?

Journal

In your journal, describe a road trip you have taken. Explain why you took the trip and how you passed the time along the way. Describe what affected you most during the journey.

Setting a Purpose

Read to discover why Sal Hiddle set out on a two thousand-mile trip cross-country and how she passed the time along the way.

BACKGROUND

Did You Know?

Sal Hiddle, the narrator of *Walk Two Moons*, is unhappy when she and her father leave their Kentucky farm for the city of Euclid, Ohio. Unlike the fictional Bybanks, Euclid—like many of the locations mentioned in the book—actually exists. It is a city of about 55,000 located on the shores of Lake Erie, twelve miles from Cleveland, Ohio. In the novel, Sal complains that the houses are "all jammed together." She might have preferred the Euclid of the early twentieth century, which was a small rural community known for the table grapes its farms produced. During and after World War II, Euclid expanded rapidly. City planners kept the business and industrial sections separate from the residential parts of town. But Sal doesn't like the effect. She compares the houses to "little birdhouses in a row"!

Figurative Language: The Simile

Walk Two Moons is filled with figurative language that creates vivid pictures in readers' minds. One type of figurative language that appears throughout the novel is the **simile**. A simile uses *like* or *as* to compare two seemingly unlike things. Examples of the use of similes that appear early in the book are "My father plucked me up like a weed"; "Trouble just naturally followed them like a filly trailing behind a mare," and "sometimes I am as ornery and stubborn as an old donkey." As you read, take note of other similes that you encounter.

VOCABULARY PREVIEW

diabolic [dī′ə bol′ik] *adj.* fiendish; wicked (p. 16)

divulge [di vulj′] *v.* to make known, especially something secret (p. 16)

flinch [flinch] *v.* to draw back, as from something painful or unpleasant (p. 36)

gullible [gul′ə bəl] *adj.* easily fooled (p. 30)

huzza [hə zä′] *interj.* used to express joy (p. 20)

primly [prim′lē] *adv.* excessively precisely or properly (p. 17)

roost [ro͞ost] *v.* to perch or settle, especially for the night (p. 1)

shrapnel [shrap′nəl] *n.* fragments from an exploding shell or bomb (p. 30)

Name _____ Date _____ Class _____

Active Reading

Walk Two Moons Chapters 1–11

The story of Sal's journey west to Idaho alternates with the story she tells Gram and Gramps about Phoebe Winterbottom. Using the boxes below, describe the principal events that occur in each story. Record the details of Sal's journey in column A and those of Phoebe's story in column B. Follow the arrows to keep the events in order.

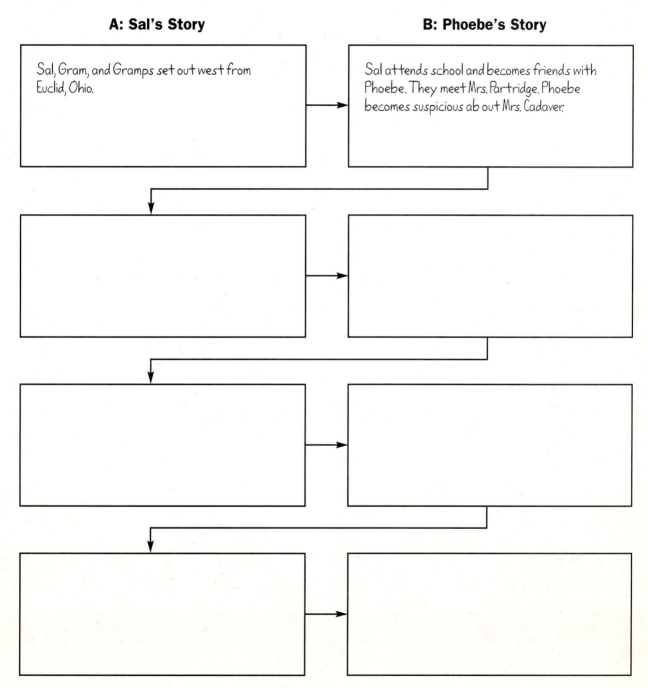

A: Sal's Story

Sal, Gram, and Gramps set out west from Euclid, Ohio.

B: Phoebe's Story

Sal attends school and becomes friends with Phoebe. They meet Mrs. Partridge. Phoebe becomes suspicious about Mrs. Cadaver.

Walk Two Moons Study Guide   17

Name _____   Date _____   Class _____

Responding
Walk Two Moons Chapters 1–11

Personal Response
What surprises you the most after reading this section?

_____
_____
_____

Analyzing Literature
Recall and Interpret

1. What reasons do Gramps and Sal's father give Sal for going on the trip? According to Sal, what are the real reasons? Why might the real reasons have been left unspoken?

   _____
   _____
   _____

2. How does Sal feel about Mrs. Cadaver? Why, do you suppose, does she feel this way?

   _____
   _____
   _____

3. What does Sal notice about Phoebe's parents that reminds her of the Pickfords, her mother's parents? Do you think she finds either couple very likeable? Explain.

   _____
   _____
   _____

4. Sal explains that the first mysterious message means that one shouldn't judge people until one has been in their shoes. Is this advice that Phoebe follows? Give reasons for your answer.

   _____
   _____
   _____

5. By the end of this section, how has the author held the reader's interest?

   _____
   _____
   _____

Name _____ Date _____ Class _____

Responding

Walk Two Moons Chapters 1–11

Analyzing Literature *(continued)*
Evaluate and Connect

6. Why, do you suppose, does Sal pass the time by telling the story about Phoebe's family? How does her experience compare to yours as described in the **Focus Activity** on page 16?

_____

_____

_____

7. What does Sal's tendency to flinch when someone touches her suggest about her character?

_____

_____

_____

Literature and Writing
Describing Characters' Behavior

Sal says that her father did not trust his own parents to behave themselves on the journey west. Imagine that he had asked Sal to write him a letter reporting on what Gram and Gramps were doing. Compose the letter that Sal might have written describing her grandparents' behavior on the drive from Euclid to Minnesota. Support the letter with incidents from the novel.

Extending Your Response
Literature Groups

The phrase *politically correct*, or *PC*, means avoiding the use of language and eliminating practices that could offend certain groups of people. The novel *Walk Two Moons* addresses the issue of political correctness in its use of the term *Native American* rather than *Indian* to refer to North America's first inhabitants. Sal does not like the sound of the term. She prefers to be called an Indian. Many Americans strive toward political correctness in their speech and behavior, but others believe that political correctness has gone too far. In your group debate the issue of whether political correctness is a value that should guide our speech and behavior.

Social Studies Connection

At the Wisconsin Dells, Gram joins a lively Native American dance. Why did the American Indians dance and what forms did their dancing take? Using the Internet or the print resources of the local library, research the significance of dancing among North America's first inhabitants. Prepare a three to five-minute presentation for the class. Enhance your presentation with the use of visual aids or sound recordings.

 Save your work for your portfolio.

Walk Two Moons Study Guide

Before You Read

Walk Two Moons Chapters 12–22

FOCUS ACTIVITY

What do you think your family and friends see when they see you? How do you see yourself? Do these views agree? Why or why not?

Web It
Create a word web with your name in the center. Off to the sides, draw circles containing aspects of your personality that other people may see. Include circles describing yourself as you really are.

Setting a Purpose
Read to discover what motivated Sal's mother to leave home.

BACKGROUND

Did You Know?
The first Europeans to arrive in North America were struck by the Native Americans' use of the calumet, or peace pipe. For many of them smoking tobacco was not recreational. They believed that the smoke rising from their pipes was a way of communicating with the spirit world. For tribes across the continent, smoking was a central part of many religious ceremonies. Indian pipes often were works of art. Their bowls were carved from soft stone. Feathers and horsehair decorated their wooden stems, which might have been more than three feet long. European settlers eagerly adopted the use of tobacco, but in their hands the custom lost its religious significance and became little more than an unhealthy addiction.

The Frame Story
A **frame story** is a plot structure that features the telling of a story within a story. The frame is the **outer** story. In most instances, it precedes and follows the **inner**, more important, story. In *Walk Two Moons*, for example, the story of Sal and her grandparents traveling across the country is the frame. While they drive west, Sal tells Gram and Gramps the story of Phoebe's family in Euclid, Ohio. This is the story within the story. But is this story the more important one? As you read about Sal's and Phoebe's adventures, decide which story is the most important.

VOCABULARY PREVIEW

anonymous [ə non′ə məs] *adj.* having an unknown author or origin (p. 46)
cantankerous [kan tang′kər əs] *adj.* bad tempered and quarrelsome (p. 54)
console [kən sōl′] *v.* to give comfort in a time of distress (p. 75)
flail [flāl] *v.* to wave about wildly, especially one's arms and legs (p. 52)
malevolent [mə le′və lənt] *adj.* doing or desiring to do evil to others (p. 44)
manna [man′ə] *n.* a miraculous gift (p. 81)
reassurance [rē′ə shoor′əns] *n.* renewed confidence or belief (p. 71)
skeptical [skep′ti kəl] *adj.* doubtful or disbelieving (p. 47)
slather [slath′ər] *v.* to spread thickly (p. 45)

Name _____ Date _____ Class _____

Active Reading

Walk Two Moons Chapters 12–22

In the diagram below find seven words that you think describe Sal. Then fill in the outer balloons with specific details that support your one-word descriptions.

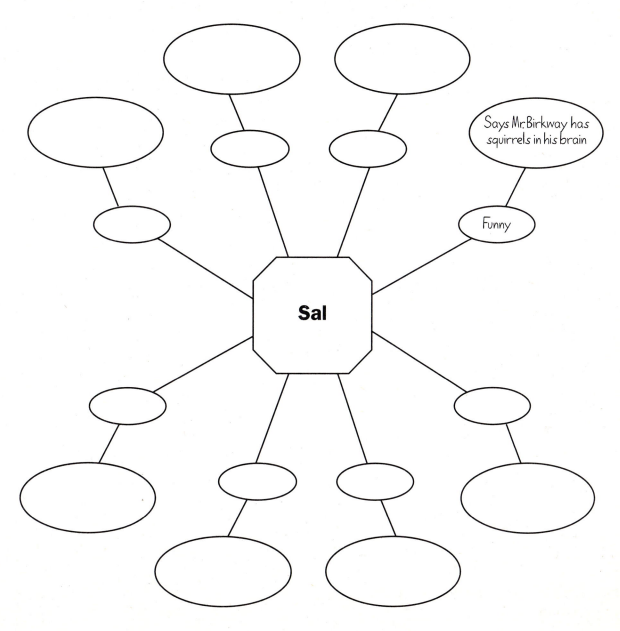

Walk Two Moons Study Guide   21

Name _____   Date _____   Class _____

Responding

Walk Two Moons Chapters 12–22

Personal Response
Which part of this section made the greatest impression on you? Why?

Analyzing Literature
Recall and Interpret

1. What is the single most precious object in Gram and Gramps Hiddle's house? What does this suggest about their relationship?

2. What does Sal understand about Mrs. Winterbottom that Phoebe and Prudence do not? What makes Sal conscious of something that Mrs. Winterbottom's own daughters are unaware of?

3. Why does hearing a bird outside the hospital remind Sal of home? Why does Gram suggest that this is "a good sign"?

4. What name does Sal's mother wish people would call her? How is this wish related to the reason she gives for having to leave the farm?

5. When Phoebe's father reads the note from his wife, Sal says, "I had a sinking, sinking feeling." What does the note say, and why does Sal react the way she does?

Name _____ Date _____ Class _____

Responding

Walk Two Moons Chapters 12–22

Analyzing Literature *(continued)*
Evaluate and Connect

6. On a scale of 1 (poor) to 10 (perfect), how would you rate the marriage of Sal's parents? Explain your choice by considering such questions as: Was it a loving relationship? Were they equal partners? Did they understand each other?

_____
_____
_____

7. Look back at the web you made for the **Focus Activity** on page 20. What can happen when the "real you" gets lost in other people's perceptions of you? How did this affect Sal's mother, do you think?

_____
_____
_____
_____

Literature and Writing
Understanding Relationships

The relationships of Sal's parents, of Phoebe's parents, and of Gram and Gramps Hiddle are important to the plot of *Walk Two Moons*. What do you think makes a successful marriage? Write a paragraph or two that describes the qualities that make Gram's and Gramps' marriage a happy one. Provide support from the novel for your opinion.

Extending Your Response
Literature Groups

Several mysteries remain unanswered at this point in the novel. They include the following:
- Who is Mrs. Cadaver?
- Who is the lunatic?
- Why is someone leaving the mysterious messages?
- Why has Mrs. Winterbottom disappeared?
- What has happened to Sal's mother?

In your group, come up with possible explanations for these mysteries. Try to reach a consensus within your group on the most reasonable explanation for each mystery.

Learning for Life

By the end of this section, Phoebe has convinced herself that her mother's disappearance is a matter for the police to investigate. Imagine that she decides to notify the police in writing, presenting all the evidence in an incident report. Compose the report that she might write. Present the facts as Phoebe sees them, using details from the novel. End the report with an analysis of what she thinks the evidence means.

 Save your work for your portfolio.

Walk Two Moons Study Guide 23

Before You Read

Walk Two Moons Chapters 23–33

FOCUS ACTIVITY

Recall an instance when you formed an opinion about someone without knowing all the facts. How did you feel when you learned the truth about that person?

Quickwrite

Recall a time when you formed an opinion about someone that turned out to be wrong. Write a brief description of why you formed the opinion and what happened that made you change your mind.

Setting a Purpose

Read to discover why Sal is forced to change her opinion of Margaret Cadaver.

BACKGROUND

Did You Know?

In the late nineteenth century, the area now occupied by the state of South Dakota was a battleground between Native Americans and European settlers. At the heart of the conflict was the beautiful Black Hills, a forested region of about six thousand square miles in the west of the territory. The Sioux people treasured this area. After much fighting and bargaining, they signed a treaty that guaranteed them possession of the Black Hills forever. This agreement lasted little more than five years, for in 1874, prospectors discovered rich deposits of gold there. White miners swarmed west, invading Indian territory in their quest for riches. The Sioux and Cheyenne fought back, winning a great victory over General George Armstrong Custer in 1876. Their resistance was futile, however, as a tide of miners and settlers swept over their land. In 1980 the U.S. Supreme Court admitted the wrong done to the Native American people. It granted them $122.5 million for the seized land. The Sioux refused the offer. They want their Black Hills returned to them. As you read about Sal's visit to the Black Hills, reflect on how special they are to many Native American people.

Appreciating Myths

A **myth** is a story whose author is unknown and that explains a people's belief about nature, an event in history, or the origin of a custom or practice. Myths usually involve gods and heroes. Myths were important both to ancient Greeks and to Native Americans because they explained occurrences in their world. As you read chapters 23–33 of *Walk Two Moons*, be alert for the myths that surface as the plot unfolds.

VOCABULARY PREVIEW

besiege [bi sēj´] *v.* to surround; crowd around; harass with questions (p. 94)
careen [kə rēn´] *v.* to sway from side to side while moving, as if out of control (p. 83)
chaotic [kā ot´ik] *adj.* totally confused or disorderly (p. 87)
crucial [kroo´shəl] *adj.* of great importance (p. 107)
miscellaneous [mis´ə lā´nē əs] *adj.* made up of a variety of ingredients (p. 87)
optimistic [op tə mis´tik] *adj.* having a positive frame of mind; hopeful (p. 87)
pious [pī´es] *adj.* devoutly religious, sometimes in appearance only (p. 110)
vaporize [vā´pə rīz´] *v.* to change or be changed into vapor; disappear (p. 121)

Name _____ Date _____ Class _____

Active Reading

Walk Two Moons Chapters 23–33

In the boxes to the left are mysteries about the world that puzzled ancient peoples. In the boxes to the right, fill in the myth that was created to answer the mystery.

Mystery: Why is the sky so high?	→	**Myth That Explains It:** People made long poles and pushed the sky high.
Mystery: Where did fire come from?	→	**Myth That Explains It:**
Mystery: Why is there evil in the world?	→	**Myth That Explains It:**

Walk Two Moons Study Guide

Name _____ Date _____ Class _____

Responding

Walk Two Moons Chapters 23–33

Personal Response
How do you feel about Mr. Birkway? Would you like to have him as a teacher? Why or why not?

Analyzing Literature
Recall and Interpret

1. What does Sal believe may have caused her mother to lose her baby? How might that belief affect Sal's feelings?

2. What does Sal see on the roof of Mary Lou's garage? Why does she say, "It made me feel peculiar" (page 92)?

3. What mystery does the myth of Pandora's box explain? Why may this story have such an effect upon Sal?

4. What story does the poem "The Tide Rises, The Tide Falls" tell? Why does Sal analyze it in class "as if it was my poem" (page 100)?

5. What does Sal learn about Mrs. Cadaver's husband? How does this alter her attitude toward Mrs. Cadaver?

26 Walk Two Moons Study Guide

Name _____ Date _____ Class _____

Responding

Walk Two Moons Chapters 23–33

Analyzing Literature *(continued)*
Evaluate and Connect

6. Phoebe is not portrayed as a likeable character in this section, yet Sal remains a loyal friend to her. Review the **Focus Activity** on page 24. What fact about Phoebe's situation influences Sal's loyalty to her?

_____
_____
_____

7. Do you feel that the author has made her a believable character? Explain your answer.

_____
_____
_____

Literature and Writing
Expressing a Viewpoint

Five mysterious messages have arrived at Phoebe Winterbottom's door. (The first four are listed on page 102; the fifth appears on page 109.) Choose one that is particularly meaningful to you and write a paragraph or two explaining why. Refer to specific incidents in your life that make it important to you.

Extending Your Response
Literature Groups

In your group, review the events that occur in this section of *Walk Two Moons*. Select two passages that are the most memorable and discuss your reasons for choosing them. Discuss the impact that the passages have had on the development of the plot.

Internet Connection

- Sal and her grandparents' cross-country trip was made possible by the U.S. Interstate Highway System, a network of nearly 27,000 miles of highways. Use the Internet to find out more about this road network and present your findings in a report to your class.
- On page 99, Sal says, referring to Mount Rushmore, "I wondered why whoever carved [the heads of the presidents] couldn't have put a couple of Indians up there too." Largely unknown to the general public is the fact that a monument to Chief Crazy Horse is being carved out of a mountain in the Black Hills just seventeen miles from Mount Rushmore. Crazy Horse was a Sioux chief whose warriors killed General Custer in the Battle of Little Bighorn. Use the Internet to find out more about the battle, Crazy Horse, and the sculpture being carved in his honor. Report your findings to the class.

 Save your work for your portfolio.

Before You Read

Walk Two Moons Chapters 34–44

FOCUS ACTIVITY

Think of an instance when you denied the truth to protect yourself. What was the situation, and why was the truth hard to accept?

Think-Pair-Share

Think of a time when you denied the truth to protect your feelings. Get together with a partner and share your experiences. What did your reactions have in common? What led you to finally accept the truth?

Setting a Purpose

Read to discover the truth that Sal has denied since the beginning of the novel.

BACKGROUND

Did You Know?

Denial is a term that describes a state of mind in which a person refuses to accept something as true. In the grieving process, for example, a survivor may simply not accept the reality that a loved one has died. Denial protects us from painful truths until we are ready to cope with them. As you read the conclusion of *Walk Two Moons*, take note of Sal's complicated feelings. Pay attention to the remarks that she lets slip about her mother's and her own behavior. Ask yourself these questions: What does Sal know about her mother? What does she want to believe? What does she still have to learn?

Climax and Resolution

In novels and stories, the **climax** is the point of greatest emotional intensity, interest, or suspense. It usually occurs at the turning point, where readers are eager to find out what happens next. The climax is followed by the **resolution**, or final outcome. This is the point where readers know or can figure out what will happen to the main characters. As you finish reading *Walk Two Moons*, look for the climax. Because there are two stories occurring simultaneously in this novel, there are two climaxes. As you wait to see what will happen to Sal at the end of her journey, you also wonder how the story of Phoebe's mother's disappearance will lend.

VOCABULARY PREVIEW

dissuade [di swād′] *v.* to persuade someone not to perform an action (p. 142)

infinitely [in′fə nit lē] *adv.* endlessly (p. 138)

mill [mil] *v.* to move around as a group without apparent purpose (p. 130)

ogle [ō′gəl] *v.* to look at with desire (p. 125)

quizzical [kwiz′i kəl] *adj.* questioning; puzzled (p. 140)

roster [ros′tər] *n.* a list of names (p. 131)

Name _____ Date _____ Class _____

Active Reading

Walk Two Moons Chapters 34–44

In *Walk Two Moons*, Sal's story and Phoebe's story are woven together. Using the Venn diagram below, write descriptive words and phrases that show how the two stories are alike and how they are different.

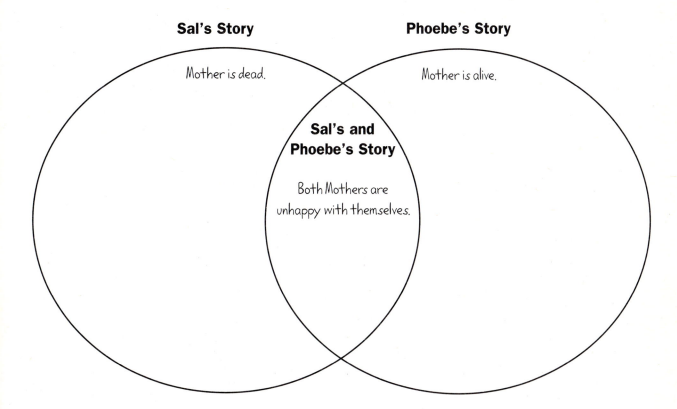

Sal's Story
Mother is dead.

Phoebe's Story
Mother is alive.

Sal's and Phoebe's Story
Both Mothers are unhappy with themselves.

Walk Two Moons Study Guide

Name _____ Date _____ Class _____

Responding

Walk Two Moons Chapters 34–44

Personal Response
Were you able to predict what Sal would find in Lewiston? How did you feel about the outcome of the novel?

Analyzing Literature
Recall and Interpret

1. What does Sal worry about as Gramps drives along the winding mountain roads? Why is she so nervous?

   _____
   _____
   _____

2. What does Sal learn about Ben's mother? How might this information bring Sal and Ben closer together?

   _____
   _____
   _____

3. Why does Mr. Winterbottom tell his wife that he doesn't think he knows her? Why does this make Sal "sad down to my bones" (p. 138)?

   _____
   _____
   _____

4. What did Sal's dog, Moody Blue, do with her puppies when they were about six weeks old? Why does this remind Sal of her mother?

   _____
   _____
   _____

5. What does Sal find in Lewiston? How does this discovery change her?

   _____
   _____
   _____

Name _____ Date _____ Class _____

Responding

Walk Two Moons Chapters 34–44

Analyzing Literature (continued)
Evaluate and Connect

6. Might it have been better if Sal's father had taken her with him when he first went out to Lewiston? Explain.

_____
_____
_____

7. Review your **Focus Activity** on page 28. How does Sal's denial of the truth compare with your example of denial? Did you find her reaction to her mother's death understandable? Give reasons for you answer.

_____
_____
_____

Literature and Writing
Understanding Character
What is the most important lesson that Sal learns at the end of *Walk Two Moons*? In a paragraph or two, discuss the most important lesson that she learns that has made her a different person than she was at the beginning of the novel.

Extending Your Response
Literature Groups
Several themes run through *Walk Two Moons*. In your group, discuss the themes that you consider important in the novel. Select two themes that you can all agree upon and express each one, using the following phrases: "*Walk Two Moons* tells us that . . .We know this because . . ." Complete the phrases by giving specific reasons. Present your statements of theme to the class to determine whether the class arrived at the same conclusions.

Learning for Life
Imagine that a movie version of *Walk Two Moons* is being produced and that you have been chosen to design the advertising poster. What image would you select to catch the eye of a passerby? What brief description of the book would accompany your photo or visual art? Create a poster that you feel captures the spirit of the novel.

 Save your work for your portfolio.

Walk Two Moons Study Guide 31

Name _____ Date _____ Class _____

All My Relations
Linda Hogan

Before You Read
Focus Question
What are some of the activities that you participate in to feel a closer connection with nature?

Background
The ceremony of the sweat lodge is observed by Native Americans across the United States. Techniques may differ, but the principle is the same: participants gather in a small structure that is heated with steam or an open fire. Smoking tobacco often plays a part in the ritual. Native Americans participate in the ceremony to communicate with the spirit world and to gain inner peace.

Responding to the Reading

1. Why does the author visit an Indian household at the opening of the essay?
   _____
   _____
   _____

2. What is the author required to bring to the ceremony?
   _____
   _____
   _____

3. What does the phrase *all my relations* refer to? Why is it an important part of the ceremony?
   _____
   _____
   _____

4. Near the end of the essay the author writes, "There is no real aloneness." What does she mean by this statement, do you think?
   _____
   _____
   _____

5. **Making Connections** The author explains that telling one's story is crucial to healing. How does this relate to the healing process Sal undergoes in *Walk Two Moons*?
   _____
   _____
   _____
   _____

Celebrate the Natural World
Native Americans believe that humans should exist in a harmonious relationship with the spirits of the natural world. Choose a living thing that is special to you—a tree, a flower, or an animal—and celebrate its existence in a poem, song, story, or picture. Try to capture what it is about this life form that excites your imagination or relates to your life.

Name _____ Date _____ Class _____

Rev. Peter Rosen

from Pa-ha-sa-pah or The Black Hills of South Dakota

Before You Read
Focus Question
Think of a place that is very special to you. How would you react if it were taken away from you?

Background
In 1875 the Black Hills of South Dakota became the center of a gold rush, transforming the area from a peaceful wilderness to part of America's "Wild West." With the arrival of the railroad, the face of the region changed forever. In 1880 the population of South Dakota was around 82,000. Ten years later it stood at 348,600. This account, written in 1895, looks back at its earlier days.

Responding to the Reading

1. How did the Black Hills change between 1875 and the time that the author describes in his account? What new technology helped bring about this change?

   _____

   _____

2. What effect does the author create by listing the wildlife that once abounded in the region?

   _____

   _____

   _____

3. How did the Native Americans feel about the white men? What myth did they tell that revealed their emotions?

   _____

   _____

   _____

4. In what way do the Badlands resemble a city?

   _____

   _____

5. **Making Connections** Recall Sal's reaction to the Black Hills when she visits with Gram and Gramps. How would you compare her feelings to those of the Native Americans described in this selection?

   _____

   _____

Learning for Life
Mount Rushmore, a monument dedicated to four American presidents, is located in the Black Hills. Sal thinks that "the Sioux would be mighty sad to have those white faces carved into their sacred hill." Using information from the novel and from this selection, design a monument that would represent the Native American point of view. Mount your design on a poster and present it to the class, explaining the ideas that led to its creation.

Walk Two Moons Study Guide

Name _____ Date _____ Class _____

E. E. Cummings
Henry Wadsworth Longfellow

the little horse is newlY *and* The Tide Rises, the Tide Falls

Before You Read
Focus Question
Recall a time when everything seemed perfect with the world and another when life seemed sad. What influenced your emotions on these occasions?

Background
The two American poems in this selection are very different in appearance. Henry Wadsworth Longfellow (1807–1882) wrote in a conventional poetic form, but E. E. Cummings (1894–1962) completely disregarded punctuation, syllable breaks, and capitalization. (His use of lower case letters began when a college anthology accidentally printed his name as *e.e. cummings*.) Cummings poems may look strange, but with careful reading they often make perfect sense.

Responding to the Reading

1. In "the little horse is newlY," how would you describe the little horse's world? How do you think he feels about it?

   _____
   _____
   _____

2. Do you think people ever experience life the way the little horse does? Explain.

   _____
   _____

3. In "The Tide Rises, the Tide Falls," what happens to the traveler? Explain how you know this.

   _____
   _____
   _____

4. How is the world revealed in "The Tide Rises, the Tide Falls" different from that described in "the little horse is newlY?"

   _____
   _____

5. In *Walk Two Moons*, Sal is struck by both of these poems when Mr. Birkway reads them to the class. What in Sal's experiences and personality might make them meaningful to her?

   _____
   _____

Performing
With a partner, choose a side of Sal's personality that is reflected in these poems. One side should be the optimistic "little horse"; the other the unfortunate "traveler." Look for passages of dialogue in the novel that capture each of these sides to Sal's personality. Perform monologues based on the passages.

Name _____ Date _____ Class _____

Lorenzo Baca
Alonzo Lopez

Five Rounds *and* Celebration

Before You Read
Focus Question
Why might the circle be considered a universal symbol?

Background
Lorenzo Baca and Alonzo Lopez are Native American poets from New Mexico. Lopez's "Celebration" is a **conventional poem** written in verse. Baca's "Five Rounds" are **concrete** poems, poems in which the words form a distinct shape. In concrete poetry, the shape contributes to the poem's overall meaning.

Responding to the Reading

1. Read "Five Rounds" carefully. Which poems could be written out as complete sentences with periods at the end?

   _____
   _____
   _____

2. What do you notice about the wording of "Five Rounds?" Why, do you suppose, did the author write them as circles?

   _____
   _____
   _____

3. How would you describe the mood of "Celebration?" What words does the poet use to convey this feeling?

   _____
   _____
   _____

4. What does the dance described in "Celebration" have in common with "Five Rounds?" What else do these poems have in common?

   _____
   _____

5. **Making Connections** In *Walk Two Moons*, Sal describes the Navaho myth of Estsanatlehi, "a woman who never dies. She grows from baby to mother to old woman and then turns into a baby again" (page 154). How does Estsanatlehi's story relate to the poems in this selection?

   _____
   _____

Choreograph a Circle Dance
Many cultures perform traditional dances that resemble a circle in form and movement. Choose a suitable theme for a circle dance. Form a group and choreograph the dance. Perform it for your class.

Name _____ Date _____ Class _____

Chaim Potok | # Moon

Before You Read
Focus Question
What material advantages of being an American do you take for granted? Why?

Background
The short story *Moon* is based on a true story about a Pakistani youth who was sold into labor to work in a carpet factory. At the age of ten, he escaped and began a campaign in the United States and Europe to free the thousands of children enslaved in Pakistan's many factories. When he returned to his homeland, he was shot down in a village. His murder was never solved.

Responding to the Reading

1. Name two things that make Moon angry. How does he attempt to control his anger?

   _____
   _____

2. What does Ashraf say that captures Moon's attention at the school assembly? Why, do you suppose, does he respond this way?

   _____
   _____

3. What change comes over Ashraf when he plays Moon's bongos? What might be a reasonable explanation for this change in him?

   _____
   _____

4. What did you learn about Moon by the end of the story?

   _____
   _____

5. **Making Connections** Sal learns the importance of walking two moons in someone else's moccasins. How does Moon learn the same lesson?

   _____
   _____

Internet Connection
In many parts of the world, children work long hours for very little pay under intolerable conditions. Conduct an Internet search to find out about child labor abuses. A key word search on *child labor* or *children's rights* will produce many sites for your research. Based on what you learn, write a report on this issue and present it to your class.

Name _____ Date _____ Class _____

TEST: *Walk Two Moons*

Recall and Interpret (40 points total; 4 points each)

A. Write the letter of the best answer.

_____ 1. Sal prays to trees on her journey west because
    a. she doesn't believe in a Supreme Being.   **c.** Gramps suggested that she should.
    b. a tree was nearly always nearby.   **d.** her middle name is Tree.

_____ 2. Who wrote the name *Chanhassen* in new cement on a brick wall?
    a. Phoebe Winterbottom   **c.** Sal
    b. Gram   **d.** Sal's father

_____ 3. Before Sal reaches her destination, Gram dies from a
    a. stroke.   **c.** car accident.
    b. snake bite.   **d.** heart attack.

_____ 4. Sal and Phoebe visit the university in order to
    a. spy on Ben.   **c.** confront the lunatic.
    b. find Mr. Winterbottom.   **d.** do some research for Mr. Birkway.

_____ 5. Over the course of the novel, Sal's state of mind moves from
    a. jealousy to rage.   **c.** peace to confusion.
    b. anger to acceptance.   **d.** sorrow to suspicion.

B. Write a short answer for each question below.

6. What explanation does Sal's father give for wanting to leave the farm? How does Sal react?

_____
_____
_____

7. When Sal tells her father that she doesn't want to know about Mrs. Cadaver, she is suddenly reminded of Phoebe. Why?

_____
_____
_____

8. What do trees taste of to Sal? Explain your answer.

_____
_____
_____

9. What does Mr. Winterbottom do that Sal thinks is noble when his wife returns with Mike?

_____
_____
_____

10. Why does Sal not look too closely at the singing tree near her mother's grave in Lewiston?

_____
_____
_____

Name _____ Date _____ Class _____

Evaluate and Connect (60 points total; 30 points each)

C. Answer two of the following essay questions on a separate sheet of paper.

1. In the following passage, from the last chapter of *Walk Two Moons*, Sal explains the importance of her trip out west. Why does she describe it as a "gift?" What did she come to understand about her mother along the way that allowed her to accept the truth?

   One day I realized that our whole trip out to Lewiston had been a gift from Gram and Gramps to me. They were giving me a chance to walk in my mother's moccasins—to see what she had seen and feel what she might have felt on her last trip (p. 153).

2. An important lesson Sal learns is that things are not always what they seem to be. Choose any two characters or incidents in the novel and describe how they appear at first to Sal. Then describe what she later learns to be true.

3. Sal tells Phoebe's story to entertain Gram and Gramps on the drive west. As the journey progresses, however, it becomes clear that Sal is learning something from her narrative. How does thinking about Phoebe's predicament open Sal's eyes about her own loss?

4. On one occasion, Mr. Birkway gives his class a lesson on **symbols**—things, people, or events that can be understood on more than one level. For instance, Mr. Birkway points out that dark, snowy woods in a poem can be merely woods on one level, but that they might also represent death or beauty. Explain how symbols are used in this novel by discussing the meanings of two of the following symbols: the singing tree, the marriage bed, and the fireplace behind the wall. Support your answer with details from the novel.

5. The following passage, from a review of *Walk Two Moons*, appeared in Booklist, November 15, 1994. In it the reviewer both praises and criticizes aspects of the novel. Explain the extent to which you agree or disagree with these remarks, supporting your answer with examples from the novel.

   The novel is ambitious and successful on many fronts: the characters, even the adults, are fully realized; the story certainly keeps readers' interest; and the pacing is good throughout. But Creech's surprises—that Phoebe's mother has an illegitimate son and that Sugar is buried in Idaho, where she died after a bus accident—are obvious in the first case and contrived in the second. Sal knows her mother is dead; that Creech makes readers think otherwise seems a cheat."